DIVORCE-LIMITED

Re-Evaluate, Repair & Rebuild your Foundation

Jasmine Carey-Crowner

Dedication

God, I thank you for your grace, discernment, guidance, and love. These are your words to your people. It is an honor to know that I am an essential vessel being used for your glory.

To Elwin, thank you for being everything I never knew that I needed. I look forward to doing life with you and continuing to help each other grow individually and collectively. We were created for each other. Let's get ready to show the world exactly what God had up His crisp white sleeve. I love you!

To my boys, CMC1 & CMC2, thank you for fueling me every step of the way. You both love me in ways I have never experienced, and I love you both as unique as you were created. I pray that my drive encourages you both to know that there is so much potential just waiting to be released. Never stop being amazing! Never stop trusting God!

To my family, thank you for encouraging me, praying for me, and pushing me to be the best version of myself. I love you all!

To my Sister-Friends. You know who you are, and you know what you mean to me. Thank you for being my Aaron and Hur and keeping me lifted when I could not find the strength.

Last, but certainly not least. To my angel who has always supported me in everything. Kejuan. I love you. I promised you I would never take my gifts to my grave and I plan to keep that promise. I did it, bro! I hope I am making you proud!

CONTENT

"The Foundation"

Chapter 1 - Re-Evaluate

Chapter 2 - Repair

Chapter 3 - Rebuild

The Final Declaration

Reflections

About the Author

DIVORCE-LIMITED

Re-Evaluate, Repair & Rebuild your Foundation

"The Foundation"

April 06, 2018 was the day that a permanent title was placed on our marriage. "Divorce-Limited" will forever be what you see when you search the records in our local court system. However, when you see us today, you would never know that our marriage had been labeled as such. Here we are, two years later, another child added to our amazing family and better than we have ever been. How? Because WE decided that WE would determine our title and the status of our marriage. "Divorce-Limited", for us, meant that divorce CAN be limited if you do your part. It meant that we COULD decide that we wanted something better and work hard at it. It meant that we were NOT required to be a statistic. However, we first had to figure out how we got to that point.

Foundation, by definition, is the lowest load-bearing part of a building, typically below ground level. Often you hear that you are only as strong as your foundation, and, in relationships, that is undoubtedly true. So, we had to do what I like to call a "Relationship Inspection." If you know anything about the home buying process, you understand how important the inspection is. Simply put, this is where you check for structural damage and see what needs to be re-evaluated, repaired, or rebuilt. And those three steps are EXACTLY what we needed to do for our marriage. Re-evaluate how we were doing things, repair what could be fixed, and completely replace or rebuild certain things that could no longer occupy a space in our relationship for us to work.

According to society, we had already done things "out of order". After just two years of being in a relationship, we welcomed our first child. I was 24 years old, on the 24th of the month, 24 weeks pregnant, and could not tell you 24 things about being a parent. When I say, we were WINGING it, My Lord! A year later, my husband deployed. It was his second deployment, but the first since we had been together. Three days before he left, we had the bright idea of getting married. If you know anything about Military forms, having to fill out ONE more form about my child who was "born out of wedlock" was going to send me overboard. So, we thought, why not? We were already engaged, and the big wedding was set for when he returned. Why not make it easier on ourselves, right?! WRONG! We knew absolutely nothing about marriage and more importantly, other than the fact that we slightly loved each other (listen, I am trying to be as open as possible here!), we did not even really know each other if I can be perfectly honest.

We knew that we loved each other, which sounded incredibly good, but what did "LOVE" look like to us? Understanding your foundation clarifies whether you realize it or not; you both come into the relationship with an idea of how things should be based on what you were taught or witnessed. You either choose to follow the example you see or decide to do the opposite in the hopes that you will never turn out like the examples set. Because we never actually discussed marriage or our upbringings in detail, we spent a lot of time trying to push our ideas on to the other person. If we had properly set the foundation for our marriage, we would have seen that neither of our upbringings were the example to follow and neither of us knew what healthy love looked like. Based on our upbringings, love and happiness looked like infidelity, yelling, mental abuse, insecurity, abandonment, dishonesty, and disrespect. So, what would you guess our foundation, subconsciously, was built on? You got it! Infidelity, yelling, mental abuse, insecurity, abandonment, dishonesty, and disrespect.

A year later, when he returned from deployment, we attended a "Yellow Ribbon Ceremony." This gathering is where soldiers and their immediate families come together to complete a series of workshops and activities related to deployment preparation or education on life after returning from deployment. Though it was a nice weekend, I must say, I left feeling very uneasy. For me, it was a weekend of hearing, "your spouse just got back from a year at war, don't stress them out. Do EVERYTHING you can to make them comfortable." Meanwhile, I had experienced multiple changes while he was gone, but had no support or anyone telling the soldiers how to treat us. While he was gone, I learned how to truly be a parent, moved out on my own, joined a new church, lost some friends, gained others, and was in a completely different space. I could not bother him with any of that though, because that would stress him, and I did not want to do that because I was told not to. So, here I was, a completely different person than who he left, and I was extremely afraid to tell him.

For the next two years, yes, years, we tolerated each other. I say tolerated each other because I soon learned what we were doing was far from love, we simply tolerated each other. We laughed, had great times, and made great memories; however, we were making absolutely no progress as far as our relationship was concerned. I had a newfound definition of what marriage was supposed to look like, based on the church, and what I had, looked nothing like it. I had been in church my entire life, but I still went off what I SAW. This time around, I wanted the type of marriage God intended for me to have. There was just one problem. It appeared to me that he had NO interest in what God was revealing to ME about our marriage. Everything was fine in his eyes, I was the unhappy one, so I needed to get happy. Then, here they came again, Orders to Deploy. Great, just what we needed, time away from each other when we were already very disconnected. December 2016, we celebrated his birthday and upcoming departure and a couple of months later he was on the other side of the world again. But it was all good, we "loved" each other, right?

Thanksgiving Day 2017, he walked through the door of my aunt's house and, though I was incredibly surprised to see him and happy that he was home safe, the rest of my excitement was very much fabricated. I was unhappy in my marriage, and I was not satisfied with myself or anything. I could not take it anymore. A couple of months later, I told him he had to leave. I did not care about his feelings, I knew I was unhappy, and so he had to go, period! So, he moved out and we worked out arrangements for our son. "But, what about what this will do to your child?" "He needs both of his parents.", "You can work this out. Nothing he did was bad enough for you to separate." I heard it all. In my mind, my parents split almost around the same age, and I turned out great. (I did not, but that is another topic for another book!) So, we separated. We did not argue or fuss. We did not even really communicate at all, to be honest. I was doing me, and he was, well, I do not know what he was doing, but I was doing me. I was making ME happy. I was doing everything that "Jasmine" wanted to do and what she felt like she missed out on over the last seven years of the relationship. Even at that point in my "happiness," I still told myself that I would not completely end things unless we tried everything. So, we went to counseling.

After three sessions, I had already made up my mind that I was correct in thinking we should just get divorced. We had a system that worked as far as our son, we were not arguing, and we attempted counseling. In my mind, everything was going the way that God intended for it to go. Sure, everything else in my life was falling apart, but I could just pray for God to work that out. After all, my husband did not care anything about church so he COULDN'T have been the man that God made for me anyway. Or so I thought.

I believed all these things until one Sunday; I went to the altar to pray. Usually, I prayed with my family, but for whatever reason, I went alone that week. As I began to pray, I heard God clear as day say: "Stop using me as an excuse for the fact that YOU don't want to grow. YOU got yourself into this mess. This was YOUR free will. I never said that man was not for you, I said the WAY he was there was not up to you. I placed him there for a purpose and you used him for your good. If you had allowed him to be in your life in the way I intended him to be none of this would be happening. You attempted to take control of everything that I could have used to bless you and you turned it into a big mess. Your role as a mother, your role as a wife, everything. Stop asking me to bless YOUR mess." I came back to my seat from prayer, completely broken. I cried so hard I could not even focus on the sermon because I was just a mess. Oh, but wait, there was more. THEN, God reminded me that the believing wife brings holiness to her marriage. While I was using him not being in church or drawing nearer to God as an excuse, I was completely bypassing one significant fact. This was, in part, MY responsibility to foster that relationship. Lord, what have I done?!

At that moment, I realized that not only was I blocking MY blessings, but I was also blocking my husband's as well. I was searching for "happiness and love" for myself and within myself. Remember what I told you regarding my perception of what happiness and love looked like; infidelity, yelling, mental abuse, insecurity, abandonment, dishonesty, and disrespect. So ultimately, for the duration of our separation, I found myself being unfaithful to who I was. I yelled at myself, mentally talked down to myself, and tried to hide my insecurities in a false idea of happiness. I tried to abandon my family because I was dishonest with myself, and overall, I became disrespectful to God in how I used him for my convenience. This was my foundation, this was our foundation, and it had now shown back up in our separation. If I had been honest when he returned from his first deployment, maybe things would be different. If he were honest with himself that he was not ready for marriage, perhaps things would have been different. If we were honest with each other instead of pretending to be happy, maybe everything would have been different. Nonetheless, here we were, eight years into our relationship, five years into our official union, one child, and BOOM…, "Divorce-Limited." So, we had to ask a question. Do we Re-Evaluate, Repair, or Rebuild? God answered and said: "if you want a new foundation that will withstand it all, do all three. But, this time, do it with ME."

I believe that divorce is the result of two possible things; 1) You were never supposed to be married, to begin with (either because of the timing or you aligned yourself with the wrong person); 2) You did not put in the work. In this book, you will learn not only how those three steps (Re-Evaluate, Repair & Rebuild) looked for us, but how it can also look for you. You can always start over. You do not need anyone's permission to decide that you want to be better or do better. You also do not need a new year or a new month to have a fresh start. Most of all, remember that things do not have to be in a horrible place for you to want to make changes. You do not have to wait for the car to break down before you consider getting an oil change. Do it today, do it now. This book is, as the gaming systems say, "Rated E for Everyone." So, grab your sledgehammer and let's get to work. It is time to Re-Evaluate, Repair, and Rebuild. Enjoy!

CHAPTER 1

Re-Evaluate

Who Are You?

The process of Re-evaluation is split into two parts. Re-evaluate yourself first then re-evaluate your relationship. A common misconception in relationships is that you are supposed to do everything 50/50 and complete the other person. A healthy relationship involves two very WHOLE people who are looking to complement each other, not complete each other. What is the difference? I am glad you asked. Complement, as a verb, means add to something in a way that enhances or improves it. Complete, by definition, is to finish making or doing. If I am looking for someone to complete me, that insinuates that I am somehow not finished. Meaning there is a void you are filling. Which suggests that if you leave me, I will need someone else or something else to fill that space for me to be made whole. Respectfully, no thank you! Therefore, it is crucial to make sure that you are already complete so that whoever comes around will only be complementing you. If they are no longer in the picture, you are still whole. Re-evaluating yourself means to get yourself back or to finally find your complete "you". You cannot discover WHY you do what you do until you know who YOU are.

It is extremely easy to point out what someone else is doing wrong but when you must begin to make changes within yourself a lot of us tend to turn a blind eye. The most challenging reality for some of us is coming to terms with the fact that we are the cause of many of our issues. It is natural to point the blame to others automatically. "Maybe if you were raised like me, things would be better. I wish you would see things my way!" "You never take me anywhere. We never do anything!" "You never call me beautiful anymore." "The only thing I am good for to you is sex because that's all you ask for." Oh yea, we go there! Now, let us re-evaluate each of those statements to see just how we may be our problem at times. I am going to rewrite each statement with a different perspective.

"Maybe if you were raised like me, things would be better" = "I would rather stay comfortable in my dysfunction than to accept that my upbringing wasn't the best because then I will have to question every part of my life and all that I know to be true. So, let us change YOU instead!"

"You never take me anywhere. We never do anything." = "I have grown bored with where we are in our relationship and would like to spice things to keep things fresh."

"You never call me beautiful anymore." = "I am feeling insecure about the weight I have put on since we got married and I no longer feel beautiful. Since having our children, I don't have the time I used to have for my self-care."

"The only thing I am good for to you is sex because that is all that you ask for." = "In past relationships this was not as important to me, however, in marriage, I desire to connect with you intimately on a level that is not just physical because I believe I have much more to offer."

For me, re-evaluating meant that I first needed to change all my "You" statements to "I" statements. The reality is that no one can make you a doormat unless you stand in front of them and lay down. No one has the power to offend you, offense is something you choose to accept. I was looking for my husband to make me whole when in fact that was my job. Finding my joy… was my job. Finding my purpose… was my job. My inability to find satisfaction in what he was able to do for me was my problem. I was looking for him to complete me. Once I re-evaluated myself, my outlook on a lot of those topics changed. To do that, I had to ask myself a series of questions. Some of those were harder to answer than others but they all were necessary for my growth. I had to make sure that I was whole on my own so that when I went back to fix my marriage, I would not still be looking for him to complete me. If I was already complete, then anything our marriage gave me was simply an enhancement. Here are some of the questions I asked myself:

Who do you know that you are? Are you satisfied with who you are? What are you most passionate about? How have your titles changed you as a person? How do the traumas from your childhood affect how you interact and think as an adult? What soul ties have you created in your past that have now made it impossible for you to have healthy relationships? Who do you have around to hold you accountable and to correct you, in love, at any time? What generational curses have you made it your personal goal to break? Who taught you how to love and what were you taught? What are 3 things you do well and in what 3 areas can you improve?

It is not a long list of questions; however, the answers will take you to an intense place if you choose to be honest with yourself. As you were reading my sample questions, I can only imagine how your mind began to wonder. Take this time to write out some questions or thoughts that you came up with on your own.

_____

_____

_____

_____

_____

_____

_____

_____

_____

I want to touch a little more in-depth on two of my sample questions because it is necessary. First, who do you know that you are? Though the answer to this will evolve as you evolve if you do not know who you are, how will you truly understand what you need to re-evaluate? Preferably, I would also like you to make sure that list does not include titles. I know that you are a mother. I know that you are a wife. I know that you are a minister, but who are YOU. When those titles are stripped, what do you have left to say about yourself? Now, before you pull out the commonly used scripture by women to describe yourself, let me stop you. I know, I know. You are "fearfully and wonderfully made". Great, thank you. Now, do you KNOW that? Because the question was "who do you KNOW that you are" not "what have you HEARD you are". So, when you answer that question, only list the descriptions you believe. God cannot bless who you pretend to be. All your answers may not be positive and that is ok. You may not have any answers at all and that is fine as well. This is just the beginning of the process. Sit in the truth of who you are long enough to realize who you want to be. Repair is soon to come!

I also wanted to go deeper regarding another subject that was mentioned in the sample questions. Soul Ties. For those that are aware of this issue, you probably avoided THAT topic like the plague. But if you do not, I will explain. First let me say that not all soul ties are bad. Soul Ties are formed when our soul (mind, will, emotions) become connected to someone or something. In unhealthy Soul Ties, parts of our soul are shared with another soul. This opens a doorway for whatever they are involved in spiritually to be passed over to you and vice-versa. This can allow bad spirits to enter. When situations that lead to adultery and/or fornication come into play, a soul tie is usually what leads to that connection you have a hard time trying to break with that person no matter how long it has been or how hard you try. It can happen in such a subtle way that you do not even really notice it. Something as simple as a song that played in the background when you were cheating or seeing the street name that they live on could bring up the smallest memory. It may seem small, but it is due to a soul tie that you have with that person. You think nothing of it until that moment you are being intimate with your spouse and they cut on the same song. Then, suddenly it happens. You are now picturing yourself with someone else and, unexpectedly, that small memory becomes a slightly bigger deal. Therefore, it is vital to heal in those areas and break those Soul Ties before attempting to join yourself with someone else.

Now, before we move any further, I invite you to give yourself some grace. If you cannot find any to give, be reminded of 2 Corinthians 12:9. God reminds us that His grace is all that we need, and His power works best in weakness. Now is NOT the time to feel inadequate or imperfect. God's word literally just told you that He works best where you fall short. His grace can cover your infidelity. His grace can cover you lashing out in anger. His grace can cover your constant need to compare yourself to the next person. God found YOUR weakness necessary enough to place HIS power in it. What you have been replaying in your mind as the thing that makes you unqualified, God says it is sufficient for His power. Just stop for a moment, clear your mind of any other distractions, and think about what that means. If God finds your weaknesses significant enough to place His power in them, imagine what He can place inside of your strengths. Imagine God taking what you were already great at and placing His power in it. My God! I know this may have seemed redundant as you were reading but I needed you to really process that point. The thought alone should stir something up in you. Ok, ok, let me move on or else I will never finish this book!

Who are We?

If you want a relationship that you never had, you must ask questions that you never asked. Re-evaluating your marriage sometimes means that you must go back to the beginning. You will find that specific issues you currently have result from situations from before your actual wedding. At some point in this part of the process, a sit-down, face-to-face, uninterrupted conversation will be necessary. However, give yourself time to process the answers separately first. These were some of the things we had to consider. Take a moment to think these questions through:

Knowing what you know now, were you "ready" for marriage when you said, "I Do"? What values do you base your marriage on? Do you believe in Gender Roles? What are your non-negotiables? What do you bring to the relationship? What do you need from the relationship? In what areas are you strong? In what areas could you improve? Did you bring hurt from past relationships of ANY kind into this relationship? What role do you play in your family (with parents, siblings etc.) and how does that affect your marriage? What are the top 3 important things in a marriage to you? What are the top 3 important things in life to you? What are your religious beliefs? In what ways does your circle (closest group of friends) influence you within your marriage and how do they hold you accountable? Again, I want to give you the time needed to write out any questions or thoughts that came to mind.

_____

_____

_____

_____

_____

_____

_____

_____

_____

There are hundreds of other questions that we could ask, but this list gives a good general starting point for re-evaluating what is most important. Typically, these questions will lead to a series of other questions that will help you to better understand yourself & your spouse. So, do not feel obligated to only stick to this list. Form fit your list of questions to whatever will help you get to the root of YOUR foundation. I strongly recommend answering these questions separately before coming together to discuss your answers. This will take away the pressure of feeling like you must have an answer immediately. Some of these questions will require deep thought. Give yourself time to make sure you can be as open and honest as possible with your answers.

Having a counselor, therapist, or mentor is also highly recommended. It is always good to have someone who can give you honest feedback about yourself. I would even consider going over your answers to these questions with that person before taking them back to your spouse. I have found that often we put things on our non-negotiable list instead of admitting that we need to change our mind frame in that area, or we have an unhealed area that topic touches on. For example, let us say drinking alcohol is a non-negotiable for you. When you talk to someone about what negative feelings you have regarding drinking, you may realize that the trauma associated with drinking is from seeing your Dad drink and become abusive. You have no problem with your spouse drinking. What you have is fear that the same actions you associate with drinking will be repeated by your spouse when they drink. That is an area that needs healing. Your spouse should not have to pay for the mistakes of your Father. However, they should be open as to whether they can give that up while you heal. Having someone who can walk you through that process is key.

One vital point to note for our married couples is that, as your relationship dynamics change, so will the answers to these questions. Changes in your environment, careers, health, family etc. can all play a crucial role in a shift in the atmosphere of your relationship. For this reason, it is important to always stay in constant communication with your spouse. You may find yourself asking these same questions multiple times and having a different answer every time. You may even realize that you do not have an answer at all. AND THAT IS OK. The ONLY correct answer is the honest answer.

Another factor to keep in mind is that, during this re-evaluation period, we must listen to understand, NOT to respond. Yes, the answers will stir up dialogue for sure. But you want to be sure that you have heard everything that your spouse had to say. Depending on where you are in your relationship, you may also be hearing some of these answers for the first time and some of them may surprise you. As a result, you want to also be sure that you have time to process what has been said so that you are capable of effectively communicating your responses.

Next, know yourself and what you can handle. Once your mood changes, so will your attitude. Your responses and interpretation may change as well. For example, if you hear an answer that makes you angry, typically everything said after that by your spouse will be received in anger and every answer you give will come from an angry, dismissive, or sarcastic space. This is not always the case, but it is extremely likely. If you feel yourself about to yell, judge, take offense or offend, ABORT MISSION! Now is NOT the time to respond! To be honest, it may be the perfect time for a break in the conversation. It is perfectly fine to say "hey, let's take a time out to process." This is to ensure that the dialogue stays healthy and productive.

It is also essential to know your spouse and what they can handle. You should never feel that you must "walk on eggshells" in your marriage. However, that does not mean that it is ok to say and do whatever you please. The point of this re-evaluation period is to reconnect and to get to the bottom of common issues. Do not bring up topics that are off-limits. If you are unaware of what those topics may be, ask. If you feel that these topics will eventually be something that needs to be discussed, encourage your spouse to seek help in those areas and not become a hindrance in your relationship. At the same time, understand that some issues are deeply rooted and may not be resolved in the way or the time frame you see fit. At that point, you should revisit those non-negotiables and see if this is something you are willing to look past for now or if you are not willing to at this moment. BE HONEST. You will be defeating the purpose of this fundamental part of the process if you are not completely honest with yourself and your spouse.

Though you will go through many emotions while in the re-evaluation period, one part can be quite scary; as you begin to share your answers, you may find yourself in a much different and unknown space. What happens if we answer all the questions and find that we no longer know the person sitting across from us? What happens if we are no longer on one accord? Does that mean that we must automatically call it quits? For some couples, that may be the case, but for most, absolutely not! I am in no way, shape, or form a relationship expert. It is also not my place to tell anyone what the fate of their relationship is. I am simply a firm believer in the idea that you should take as many steps as possible to ensure that you are making the correct decision. Any decision you make should be made with a clear heart and mind so that it does not develop into another area in life that you spend years attempting to heal from. I do not have a magic wand that I can wave around or an 8-Ball that I can shake to tell you the outcome of your relationship. What I DO have are the promises of God. One promise in particular, states that God promises to answer us. But remember, the carpenter cannot fix the broken thing that you never gave Him to fix. What do I mean by that? What I mean is that it is time to start on the next step in the process. How can God give you an answer to something you never gave over to him as a question or concern? Simply put, it is time to Repair.

CHAPTER **2**

Repair

Now that you have answered the questions in Chapter One, I would assume you have found at least SOME areas in which you must personally improve as well as improve your relationship. If you did not find any areas that you need to improve, you were not honest. That, I can guarantee! Keep re-evaluating until you can pinpoint what areas you could stand to repair. My advice is to start looking at your list of answers and begin to prioritize. I say prioritize because all the issues will need to be addressed at some point, but you should put them in order based on which situations hold you back the most from being your best you.

When we think about the word repair, we think of the ability to fix, mend, make good, or put right something that is damaged. The repair process is challenging. Certain things can be repaired, but if you are truly trying to give yourself a new foundation, it is important to know what things to improve and what to leave behind and replace. Be careful not to confuse the two, or you will end up back at square one. The other tricky part is that sometimes you do not know a thing needs to be replaced until you attempt to repair it. Discernment will be your best friend in this process. For anyone who may not know what that is, let me explain. Discernment is essentially a decision-making process in which you make a discovery that can lead to future action. In a spiritual sense, God guides you in helping to ensure that you arrive at the best decision. So before repairing anything, I would first go into deep prayer and ask God to reveal what areas He wants to fix and what He wants to replace. Again, if you want something you never had, you must do things in ways you have never done. For me, God's way is the best.

Get Uncomfortable

One of the things my friends love to hate about me is that I am constantly reminding them to get uncomfortable. It is imperative when repairing that you step outside of the situation for a while. Many of the messages we are waiting for from God are missed because we cannot hear them. If you are trying to hear from God about being debt-free, but you stay comfortable around many friends who always encourage you to spend money frivolously, how much change will come from that? If you are trying to hear from God about changing your unfaithful ways but insist on staying around friends and listening to people who are not in a healthy space in their relationship, how much good would that be to you and your spouse? Getting uncomfortable requires you to go into a space of being on alert. If you hear that there have been armed robberies in your area, you will not be as worried about it from the comfort of your home. The second you must step outside of your house; you will be on high alert. You may have protection, watch your surroundings, and even pray more. That all sounds great until someone attacks you in the comfort of your home.

Then what is your defense? That "someone" is the enemy. We often hear that the enemy comes to steal, kill, and destroy; this is done best in the places you are most comfortable. God gave Abram a clear command in Genesis 12. The instruction was to leave his country, his people, and his Father's house and GO to the land that God would show him. What if everything God is trying to show you and change about you is somewhere in a space you have never ventured to? What if your purpose is hiding in an unknown space? What if the communication that you have been lacking in your marriage is hidden in a conversation you have been avoiding? To step toward your purpose, you must step away from your security. Go forward, knowing that God has already prepared the place that you are heading to; therefore, He is the only security you need.

Honesty

I have expressed this previously, but I feel the need to mention again that honesty will be vital as you begin to repair. Be truthful with yourself and your spouse. With honesty, you will be able to move forward and decide what to repair or replace. I will give you one example that I have seen many times. For some people, they listed infidelity as a non-negotiable. Honesty kicks in when you have to look at yourself and say, "I accepted and excused infidelity my entire relationship. Now I have a ring on my finger, and I'm expecting this person to stop something that I allowed for so long." Are you allowed to grow and see that you deserve more? Absolutely.

The issue comes in when you blame someone else for a truth you CHOSE not to accept about them. This person showed you on their own who they were. YOU believed you had so much to offer that they would change. YOU thought that if they were coming home to you, nothing else mattered. YOU felt that if you had the title, they would put you on a higher pedestal than anyone else. When telling the story of where things went wrong, most people often say: "Our relationship did not work out because they wanted to continue to cheat, and I would not allow that." HONESTY and GROWTH happen when you can say: "Our relationship did not work out because I allowed myself to believe the opposite of what I knew to be true. I accepted circumstances and treatment that I was not fully accepting of in exchange for companionship." Attached to this topic is the reality that people CAN change.

Some people get to a point where that lifestyle no longer suits them, and they now wish to grow. Now, are you honest enough to admit that you have carried trust issues into your marriage based on infidelity that you allowed or forgave previously? Are you honest enough to say that while you were waiting for them to grow, you completely ignored the change in yourself to build up a defense against the effects of the hurt? Some people never go this deep into thinking about topics, so the repair or replacement they are looking to do only touches the surface. Repair your mindset. Replace excuses with the entire truth about the situation. Dig Deeper!

Dig Deeper

Once you know what areas to repair or replace, I would encourage you to find your "WHY's" and your "HOW's". This requires you to dig deeper into the statements we sometimes make as well as the answers to the questions that you asked yourself and your spouse during the Re-Evaluation process. This will be different for everyone, but I will take one of the statements that I gave as an example to help you fully understand.

"Maybe if you were raised like me, things would be better" = "I would rather stay comfortable in my dysfunction than to accept that my upbringing wasn't the best because then I will have to question every part of my life and all that I know to be true. So, let us change YOU instead!"

There are several "why's or how's" that can be extracted from this statement; Why am I comfortable in dysfunction? How was my upbringing not the best? Why am I afraid to question my upbringing? Why is it easier for me to change others more than myself? How is changing YOU going to help ME?

Let me give you another example.

"What generational curses have you made it your personal goal to break?" Now, let us break that down. How is this a generational curse? Why have you made this a personal goal? How does this affect you in your life?

Now, refer to the "We" section of questions. "Knowing what you know now, were you "ready" for marriage when you said, "I Do"?" Ok, let us break this down as well. How does "ready" for marriage look to you? Why did you say, "I do"? Why has your opinion changed? (if it has changed)

Take some time to do that for each statement and answer you came up with and see what different things you discover. As I said, this part goes deeper into all the things you have re-evaluated about yourself. There is not much advice I can give because every single person reading this will have different answers, lifestyles and scenarios that will change the dynamic of anything I could possibly say. What I will do, is give the necessary insight on what the process SHOULD look like.

Repair

It is time to repair. For a moment, let us think of your life or your marriage as an empty lot of land. Your dream is to build a house and have a garden. You have just purchased this lot, and you plan to build here. There is one problem. At one point, due to nature running its course, all types of weeds and plants have begun to grow right where you plan to build. You have made your assessment in the re-evaluation period, but now it is time to repair it. You must pull up everything that has taken root where it does not belong so that you can start with a clean slate. Those old weeds are your past hurts, traumas, insecurities, infidelities, lies, etc. Now, attached to those weeds are some beautiful plants that managed to grow somehow. Those plants represent the happy moments, the fun memories, the blessings that you received, etc. You look at them, and you think, well, those can stay, they will make a good garden.

Suddenly you realize the roots are intertwined with the roots of the weeds. So, you have two choices. Pull up everything, the good and the bad, and start fresh. Or leave the beautiful plants and deal with the weeds while trying to hide them. My suggestion: PULL UP EVERYTHING! If you want a new foundation, sometimes you must be willing to sacrifice the good AND the bad with trust in God that whatever He has is greater than anything you have ever had. Now, it is time to dig! You will get dirty, you will possibly get some new wounds in the process, but your focus should be on the reward at the end.

Replace

You look up, and there it is, the beauty of a clean slate. The only problem is, once you have removed everything, you notice that the land is not fit to build on. You did a soil test and realized that the ground would not hold the weight of what you are building. Not just that, but it also does not absorb water well. This soil is the status of your marriage as well as your life. You can build here, however, until the soil is replaced, nothing you put on it will last. But you did not find that out until after trying to repair it. Now you ask yourself a question. What if it is good enough for the house, but not the garden? I can still attempt to put the garden there and see what will happen, right? I am going to pause here to reference The Parable of the Sower. In Matthew 13, a farmer went out to sow his seed.

As he was scattering the seed, some seeds fell along the path, and the birds came and ate it up. Other seeds fell on rocky places, where it did not have much soil. It sprang up quickly because the soil was shallow. However, when the sun came up, the plants were burned, and they withered because they had no root. Other seeds fell among thorns, which grew up and choked the plants. The seeds that fell on good soil produced a crop that was a hundred, sixty, or thirty times what was sown. A seed is only as good as the soil used to fertilize it, and the work put into it.

Do yourself a favor and REPLACE THAT SOIL. Replace those friendships that serve no purpose. Replace that mind-frame that has kept you stagnant. Replace your will with Gods' will. Replace that resentment you are holding on to from things your spouse did years ago. Replace everything that serves no purpose with the tools and resources you need to properly obtain what was promised to you. Once you have repaired everything you could and replaced everything beyond repair, you will see the beauty of your clean slate. NOW, you have permission to rebuild.

CHAPTER 3

Rebuild

The 16-Day Devotional

You have re-evaluated who you are and where you are, and you have taken steps to repair or replace in each necessary area. Now it is time to Rebuild; this the stage where you give both yourself and your spouse a clean slate and try things a different way. There are many areas to focus on when it comes to rebuilding. Because I do not want you to rush to rebuild, I encourage you to take your time through this 16-Day Devotional. I know that may seem odd but hear me out. I was very strategic in choosing that number. Eight is the number that represents New Beginnings. Sixteen is twice that, representing a second new beginning. Sixteen is also the number that represents Love and Manifestations.

For this reason, I included declarations that I would like for you to recite. They may not FEEL true as you are saying them but speak these things that are not as if they are until they manifest. These numbers were also introduced to me separately. The number 1 by itself represents individuality, but when you come together as one, it also represents unity. Six is the number of days to sow and harvest the soil. So, 16 (sixteen) can also represent what happens when a couple is united in sowing and accompanying harvest that you reap as a result. After these 16 (sixteen) days, my prayer is that you will have successfully begun to sow seeds within your new foundation and hopefully start to see the harvest as well.

One factor to keep in mind is that it took some of you years to get to this point. If you need more than one day for a topic, take the time that you need. It is more important to do this in a way that will produce the most progress. Each day includes a devotion, a prayer, and a declaration. Though I pray that you have been taking notes the entire book, I strongly encourage you to write down the declarations in a place where you can see and speak them daily. You may not believe all of these just yet, but I want you to speak each declaration with the confidence that God is renewing you in your rebuilding process. Remember, speak these things that are not as if they are so. There are lines provided for you to express how God is speaking to you each day. You can also use this space to write out scriptures, quotes, and any other declarations you feel will help you in the topics covered. Now, grab your spouses' hand and a "Cup of Grace." It is time to get ready to rebuild this foundation!

Day 1: Fasting & Prayer

Calm Down. Do not go hiding your favorite snacks! I know that as soon as you read the word "fast," you immediately thought of food. Let me reintroduce that word to you in a different way. The act of fasting releases the supernatural power of God. It is a tool we can use when there is opposition to God's will in our lives. Meaning, when something in your life is causing you to stray from what God is calling you to do, you replace it with prayer, worship, and quality time with God to get back on track. People will most commonly turn down their plates, stay off social media, give up fast foods and even television to reconnect with God. Today I want to challenge you to fast from negative words and thinking. For the remainder of this 16-Day devotional, challenge yourself to remove all things negative; this includes, but is not limited to, the following: Talking down to yourself or your spouse, offending others, being offended, feelings of inadequacy, talking yourself out of things you know you were called to do because it is "too hard" and keeping yourself around negative friends and family members.

Imagine how great your communication could be if NOTHING your spouse did ever offended you. Imagine how much peace you would have if NO ONE around you bought negative energy. Image the leaps you could take and the things you could accomplish if you never told yourself that you could not. All of this sounds amazing, I am sure. However, multiply the excitement by infinity because when you replace all those things with God, there is no limit to how great He can change your life in those areas.

With fasting, of course, comes prayer. Because this devotional will prompt you to pray, I would like to touch on one topic that I never knew was a hindrance until recently—praying without a pure heart. Psalm 66:18 reminds us that if we are holding ill feelings, sin, wickedness, etc., God will not honor that prayer in our hearts concerning a particular thing. Have you ever wondered why you did not hear an answer from God concerning a specific topic or person? Did you ever consider that before you ever prayed that prayer, God already knew how you HONESTLY felt about it and moved according to how you felt and not what you said? There is an issue that you keep praying about, and it seems like God forgot about you. He did not. What he is waiting on is for you to approach Him in prayer about the TRUE issue—your heart. Before fasting, before expecting God to move mountains on your behalf, ask God to change your heart concerning that mountain.

Today I encourage you to seek God in the topic of Fasting & Praying. Say this prayer:

Lord, I thank you for the opportunity to draw nearer to you. Please show me the things I have made idols in my life and remove anything that is not aligned with your will. Hold a mirror to my heart and allow me to see what is holding me back. Show me, me. Please save me from myself. Allow me to learn different types of prayer and worship. Remove all negativity around me that prevents me from living out my purpose. Increase my supply of "God Strength" needed to stay focused on the tasks you have given me. In Jesus' name, Amen

**Declaration: I HAVE A CLEAN HEART AND
NEGATIVITY HAS NO PLACE IN MY LIFE**

_____

_____

_____

_____

_____

_____

_____

_____

_____

_____

Day 2: Forgiveness & Healing

You must forgive yourself and your spouse daily. This will often put you in situations that cause you to forgive when you feel that you were not wrong or without full closure. The ultimate goal is to move forward in your new beginning. While on the topic of closure, let me make a pit stop. In my opinion, closure is subjective. I believe that people use the term closure but what they really mean is that they did not get THEIR way in a situation. If you feel like that in any of the areas you are having issues in, I encourage you to seek healing rather than closure. When you seek closure, you are subconsciously looking for that situation to disappear or have complete resolve. When you look to heal, you acknowledge that yes, that situation happened, but I am gaining the tools necessary not to let it affect me. If you cover an area with a bandage but never actually treat it, you risk infection as soon as something that does not belong there gets into that area. When you properly treat the area first, it takes longer, but you are no longer at risk once it is fully healed. The same applies to your life. Instead of trying to just simply put a bandage over your problems, deal with the process of healing it properly so that it no longer affects you. Forgiveness is for YOU, and nothing you do will ever change how you feel until you realize that fact. Because you are two imperfect people, you will find yourselves continually forgiving each other. Forgiveness is very much a mindset. You cannot just say that you have forgiven someone; you must possess the spirit of forgiveness for it to make an impact.

It may seem like something as simple as getting mad at your spouse for forgetting something you asked for when they went to the store. By the third time it happens, you find yourself fussing because "you NEVER listen to me." Instead of having each incident be its own, you are now mad about everything that reminds you of this situation. You cannot move forward if you are holding on to everything that ever happened. If you are focused on what went wrong, you will never appreciate the abundance of what is going right.

Today, I encourage you to seek God in forgiveness. Say this prayer:

Lord, I thank you for being a forgiving God. Forgive me for deciding on my own that I had the right to hold grudges. Your word tells me in Mark 6:15 that if I do not forgive others for their offenses, you will not forgive mine. So, I ask that you give me a spirit of forgiveness. Remove any grudges that I may be holding on to and help me to see people for who you created them to be and not from the space of judgment according to who I have made them out to be. In Jesus' name, Amen.

Your Declaration: I HAVE THE SPIRIT OF FORGIVENESS INSIDE OF ME AT ALL TIMES

_____

_____

_____

_____

_____

_____

_____

_____

_____

_____

Day 3: Mindset

You must change your mindset to Rebuild. Start by changing how you think. When things go wrong, and trust me, they will; what happens next is about 5% due to the situation and 95% how you responded to the situation. When hard times come, will you stay stagnant and give up? Or will you begin to decree and declare that things will NOT always be this way and there WILL be joy after this? It does not matter what the situation LOOKS like; what matters is what you know in your mind and your heart to be true about what God has already revealed to you. Choose to have a positive outlook on things. Instead of saying, "I got to go to work," try saying, "I GET to go to work." Instead of saying, "I have to spend time with my spouse," try saying, "I GET to spend time with my spouse." It instantly puts you in a thankful mindset, and you go from feeling obligated to feeling appreciative of the opportunity to do such things. Once you train your mind to understand that everything you have is simply a privilege, you will operate in a more humbled mindset down to the air you breathe.

Another topic that I believe is important is that comparing your marriage to someone else's will not make your marriage better. When we get in the mindset of coveting what someone else has, we lose sight of what God is doing in our situation. Repeat this until you believe it: MY healthy marriage is my goal. Not those celebrities you see on social media. Not those friends you have that seem perfect. Not even your parents who have been married your entire life. When you develop a mindset that YOUR marriage is the best, you begin to operate in a way that ensures things stay that way.

Today I want to encourage you to seek God concerning your Mind. Say this prayer:

God, I thank you for a mind and heart that continues to seek you. Forgive me for the times I took advantage of the fact that you grant me grace no matter how many times I stray in my train of thought. Your word reminds me not to be conformed to this world, but be transformed by the renewal of my mind, that by testing I may discern what the will of God is, what is good and acceptable and perfect. So right now, I ask that you renew my mind and my thoughts. Allow me to change the way that I think and remind me to keep a positive outlook. In Jesus' name, Amen.

Declaration: I DO HAVE A SOUND MIND AND POSITIVE THOUGHTS CONCERNING MYSELF AND MY MARRIAGE

_____

_____

_____

_____

_____

_____

_____

_____

_____

Day 4: Remove the Limits

As I said previously, if you want a relationship that you have never had (whether that be with yourself or others), you must do things you have never done. You must remove the limits you have placed on God. Imagine following your plans and asking God to do something for you in the next six months, but He was prepared to bless you with that exact thing in the next 6 hours had you just believed that He could. Putting limits on God not only stalls your growth, but it can also place a halt on everything that is attached to your "yes." You must believe God at the CAPACITY in which He can bless you. If you are unsure of that capacity, refer to His word. Here are a few references from scriptures to get you started:

2 Corinthians 9:8 reminds us that God can bless you, ABUNDANTLY. In ALL things, at All times, having ALL that you need, you WILL abound in every good work.

Psalm 147:5 says GREAT is our Lord and abundant in strength. His understanding is INFINITE.

Ephesians 3:20 is another excellent scripture. It reminds us that God can do IMMEASURABLY more than all we ask or imagine, according to His power that is at work within us.

Abundantly, Infinitely, and Immeasurably are three simple words. However, when you attach them to the CAPACITY, God can bless you; it should help you remove the limits you have placed on what you believe in His name. Yes, God can give you a good job. He can also put you in position for your dream job. Yes, God can restore your marriage. He can also make it brand new and bring you back together in a way you have never experienced. Yes, God can make you happy. He can also catapult you into a joy that you have never experienced. Now every room you enter is suddenly filled with nothing but the joy of the Lord. So, do yourself a favor and remove the limits you have placed on God. I promise when you begin to see His capacity, you will never be the same.

Today I encourage you to seek God concerning the limits you have placed on Him. Say this prayer:

Lord, I praise you for being a God of infinite abilities. Forgive me for putting a limit on your capacity. Your word reminds me that you can do all things abundantly, infinitely, and immeasurably. Help me to believe that you can blow my mind. Help me to believe that you can catapult me to levels I never believed I could reach. Allow me to understand who you truly are and the power that you possess. In Jesus' name, Amen.

Declaration: I DO BELIEVE GOD AT THE CAPACITY HE IS ABLE TO BLESS ME

_____

_____

_____

_____

_____

_____

_____

_____

_____

_____

Day 5: Compromise

Hopefully, during your first two phases of this book, you realized that your way may not always be the best. If you did not realize that yet, start the book over. One of the first things that I discovered during our Rebuild phase is that I needed my husband, and I needed his ways. This realization came from the topic we disagreed on the most. Money! I was a person who had no problem spending $800 on a purse and spent half of every check on new handbags, shoes, and clothes. Just for context, I was also 22 with no responsibilities. I married a man who would put back a pair of shoes if they cost more than $40. There was a compromise to be made. I had to compromise with not spending large sums of money on unnecessary items, and he had to compromise on quality over quantity. Sure, spending only $40 sounds great, but when you must constantly replace that item, you spend the same amount as what someone else did in one purchase. However, it being the most expensive does not make it the best option. See, compromise! Let me ALSO say that this was before having children and the compromise became A LOT easier when that formula rang up $50 per can. I still love to treat myself from time to time, but I have a completely different outlook on priorities.

Name some areas that you feel you and your spouse could compromise better? In what ways can you be more open to your spouses' mindset as it relates to areas you disagree with the most?

Today I invite you to seek God concerning your ability to compromise. Say this prayer:

God, I thank you for being a peacemaker. Forgive me for only wanting things to work my way. Show me how my ways are not the best and allow me to accept another option openly. In Jesus' name, Amen.

Declaration: COMPROMISE IS A NEW
NORMAL IN MY MARRIAGE

_____

_____

_____

_____

_____

_____

_____

_____

_____

Day 6: Prioritize

In life, there will always seem like there are not enough hours in the day for everything. I learned that once I only tried to make time for what I SHOULD be doing, it became a lot easier to manage. I spent hours on social media and trying to be everything for everyone and never got anything done that I was actually "assigned" to do. By that, I mean assigned by God. When you realize what is most vital in helping you to achieve the life God meant for you to have, you realize that certain things take precedence over others. Yes, I would love to make it to everything my friends and family have. However, time, money, and life will not allow that. Yes, I would love to be there in every way possible. However, I cannot take on every problem, for the sake of my mental health, as if it were my own. In the church, you are taught that your marriage is your first ministry. If your home is out of order, every other part of your life will be as well. When we realized that, we rebuilt a life in which the things that have the most impact on our growth took priority, and everything else had to fall in line.

Today I encourage you to seek God concerning your priorities. Say this prayer:

Lord, I thank you for loving me and caring for me. I desire to prioritize my life in a way that honors you. Show me how to align my life in a way that allows me to move according to your will. Show me the areas that I need to move to the bottom of my list or remove altogether. I desire to have the Holy Spirit lead me in all my ways. In Jesus' name, Amen.

Declaration: MY LIFE IS PRIORITIZED
ACCORDING TO THE WILL OF GOD

_____

_____

_____

_____

_____

_____

_____

_____

_____

_____

Day 7: Balance

In chapter 1, one of the questions I asked was, "What role do you play in your family." It may have seemed like a silly question, but it was not until I got married that I found out how important this question was. I married someone who was the only boy in his family and came from a separated family. Essentially, he was the "man" of the house. That sounds great until you get married and realize you cannot be the head in multiple places simultaneously. This caused a lot of friction because I always felt that I competed for time and status. It was a constant battle between whose opinion should be more important between myself and his family. Holidays became an issue as well. We were always in a struggle with who to spend time with. We are both products of divorced households, so there are four sides of the family for me and 2 for him. Add a child into the mix, and EVERYONE feels entitled to see this child every holiday. Talk about exhausting! The best form of balance for us was the realization that nothing would ever be evenly balanced again. We had to create a life that worked for us. Some holidays meant not seeing anyone and merely making memories with the family we created inside our household.

With balance also comes an understanding that it is unrealistic to think that your spouse is the only one in life that matters. You are each very entitled to your own separate time, either to yourself or with friends or family. There can be a balance between the life you are creating together and the life you are trying to build for yourself. We all have dreams and aspirations that are personal. It is important to remember to encourage your spouse in these areas as well. They should know that you care as much for them as a unit as you do about them as an individual. If this does not compromise your relationship in any way, having your "YOU" time is necessary.

Today I encourage you to seek God concerning how to balance. Say this prayer:

God, I honor you for being able to cover everything and everyone. Forgive me for trying to do your job. Show me what and who you have assigned to me. Stop me from trying to put too much on my plate and allow me to do what works best for my family. Remind me to encourage my spouse in areas that may not be as important to me but are still meaningful to them. In Jesus' name, Amen

Declaration: I DO HAVE BALANCE IN MY LIFE

_____

_____

_____

_____

_____

_____

_____

_____

_____

Day 8: Happy Wife, Happy Life

Ladies and Gentlemen, let me introduce you to the biggest lie ever told: "Happy Wife, Happy Life." Oh yea, I have said it myself. I even believed it for a while. It was not until I realized that my husband never being happy or fulfilled was the most selfish thing I could ever allow. It was also selfish for me to believe that he could only find happiness in making me happy. I could not even enjoy being happy when I knew that he was unhappy. One of the best things that we did during our repair phase was to find what makes us happy outside of each other. That way, when he was feeling down, I had my source to keep me going. At that point, I was also able to foster him into a state of being happy. Again, these are all my opinions. You do what works best for your relationship. But as for me and MY home, "Happy Spouse, Happy House."

Today I invite you to seek God concerning the happiness of your spouse. Say this prayer:

God, I thank you for my spouse. Forgive me for not always making both of our happiness a priority. Show me how my spouse feels and help me make the necessary changes to ensure that we are getting what we need from this marriage. In Jesus' name, Amen.

**Declaration: MY SPOUSES' HAPPINESS IS
JUST AS IMPORTANT AS MINE**

_____

_____

_____

_____

_____

_____

_____

Day 9: One Accord

We learned over time that being on one accord did not mean that we would always agree. Instead, it meant that we were two separate people with two different thoughts and opinions who had to move collectively in one direction for healthy growth in our marriage. We learned that it would not be impossible to always agree; however, we had to change HOW we disagreed. As you begin to rebuild, there is something important to remember. Disagree at home, walk out on one accord. When you have a common goal, though you have different ways and thoughts on how to achieve it, you must have ONE plan for what you are going to do as a unit to achieve it. Being on one accord also means that you and your spouse come to that decision together. If for any reason you cannot agree, tap into the source. The source is not your friends and family; the source is God. If I had an Infiniti Truck that was giving me issues, I am not going to talk to the person wearing an Infiniti shirt but has only worked on Chryslers when I have the option to speak to the maker of the Infiniti. What do I mean by that? I mean, I understand that you may have friends and family who are married, and they may have some great marriage advice, but your final decision should come from the CREATOR of companionship. What they give you will come from their experiences and what worked for them. You and your spouse were placed together for a purpose only known by God, so He is the only one who can tell you what decision to make concerning HIS will for your life.

Today I encourage you to seek God about being on one accord with your spouse. Say this prayer:

Lord, I thank you for being at the center of our marriage. Show us how to disagree in love and come together to move forward with the work you have set out for us to do. Allow us to be on one accord, not just with each other but also with your will for our lives. We give you all the glory and honor. In Jesus' name, Amen.

Declaration: I AM ON ONE ACCORD WITH MY SPOUSE AND WE ARE MOVING IN UNISON TOWARD THE WILL OF GOD FOR OUR MARRIAGE

_____

_____

_____

_____

_____

_____

_____

_____

_____

Day 10: Pick Your Battles

Please repeat after me; EVERYTHING DOES NOT WARRANT A RESPONSE OR REACTION! If you disagree with that statement, reread it until you agree. If you know that your spouse had a horrible day at work or just in general and they may be a little snappy, now is NOT the time to decide to be in your feelings and take offense. This is not about you, and eventually, they will come back and acknowledge that. For now, "Smile, Pray and Stay out of the way!". The second you choose to make it about how they are treating you, you have now created a problem where there is not one. Instead, let them cool down, and when the time is right, you can acknowledge how their attitude affected you. Give them the chance to see it on their own first. Always feeling the need to correct your spouse can stand in the way of an area where God is trying to grow them. At the same time, God may also be using their attitude to grow you in the areas of patience and understanding. Be sure to have clear instructions on what to say and when to say it before addressing anything.

Today I invite you to seek God regarding choosing your battles wisely. Say this prayer:

Lord, I thank you for my spouse and for being the creator of companionship. I ask that you give me the discernment to know when to speak and when to keep quiet. Show me what battles you have assigned to me and what battles you plan to fight on my behalf. Give me the patience to wait for your instructions before speaking. In Jesus' name, Amen.

Declaration: I HAVE THE DISCERNMENT TO KNOW WHAT BATTLES ARE MINE TO FIGHT

_____

_____

_____

_____

_____

_____

_____

_____

_____

_____

Day 11: Our Needs Change. Check-in

For years I have seen many couples stressing the importance of knowing how their partners express love. They read books, took tests, and based their every move on what they found. In our rebuilding phase, I learned that needs change. Though it sounds genuinely nice to finally know what your partner needs, tomorrow, that need may change. I have absolutely nothing against those tests. What I realized is that we would have to take it daily to get accurate results. Yes, some days I want gifts. However, I do not want you to bring me a gift on a day I only need a hug. The biggest mistake I made was trying to figure out my husband on my own. He was right there; I could have simply asked him. Instead, I took every test, read every book, and came up with an idea of who he was and what he needed. So, when his needs changed, it made no sense to me because "I knew him and what he needed." Our check-ins also lead to a significant find. There are some needs that you will not be able to meet for your spouse. Everything is not your job to fix or make right. Some things require you to work it out on your own. There is no test or book to guide you through things that are just a learning experience. You must be content that you have done your part and that some situations are simply beyond your control; if you are doing your part, that is your only responsibility.

Something interesting happened while writing this book, and it gave me a perfect example of HOW to properly check-in. We were preparing to celebrate my husband's birthday, and I stressed about it for a week, trying to decide what to get him. The day before his birthday, I still had nothing. Because of the pandemic we were in, I had to leave my job. Funds were low, and anything that I could imagine getting him cost more than what I had. Finally, I decided to give him a day off. Our 8-year-old loves to throw him an in-home birthday party every year. So, I got everything that he needed for that and headed home. We also have a tradition that every year, he gets one piece of carrot cake (our favorite). I made sure to pick that up as well.

We all ate breakfast, lunch, and dinner together, and I did not bother him with anything else for the rest of the day. At the end of the night, when we were getting ready for bed, I said, "I'm sorry that I couldn't go all out like I usually do. I wanted to do something extravagant, but funds wouldn't allow it, so I had to keep it simple." His response shocked me. He said, "Actually, this was the best birthday I have had because it WAS simple. YOU like extravagant things; I do not. It is the little things that mean the most to me. Thank you!" All this time I spent stressing, and not once did I LISTEN. I kept asking what he wanted as a gift, and he said he did not want anything. I kept asking what he wanted to do, and he said he did not want to do anything. I could have saved myself so much stress had I LISTENED during my check-in. It also made me realize that this was the 10th birthday we had spent together as a couple, and it was the only time that I did what he needed. What he needed was NOTHING.

Today I encourage you to seek God concerning the needs in your relationship. Say This Prayer:

Lord, today I thank you for clarity. Allow my spouse and I to be open and honest about what we need individually and collectively. As our needs change, help us to be honest enough to voice that to the other person. Give us the discernment to recognize that a change has happened so that we may be clear when we communicate our needs. Remind us to check-in with each other daily and to be intentional about listening to what is said. In Jesus' name, Amen.

Declaration: I HAVE THE CLEAR KNOWLEDGE
OF MY SPOUSES' NEEDS AND MY OWN

_____

_____

_____

_____

_____

_____

_____

_____

_____

_____

Day 12: Submission

Uh oh! We hate that word, don't we?! Yes, but only until we understand what it DOES NOT mean. Submission does not imply ownership. Submission does not suggest that you are a slave. Submission does not mean control. Submission does not mean that only one spouse has a say. It is often said that a wife should submit to her husband, and, biblically, that is correct. However, you are both in a place of submission. The wife submits to the husband, and the husband submits to God. Think of submission in group assignments. When you are given an assignment, once it is complete, you submit it to your teacher. The person leading has the role of turning it in, but everyone involved must do their part. I am submitting my love, loyalty, trust, and respect to my husband. At the same time, he is submitting to God.

I realized my challenge with submission began long before I became a wife. I was raised with the understanding that you should never rely on a man. No one ever taught me anything about this topic, I learned by watching the women around me. So, when it was my turn to submit, I had no idea how that was supposed to look. I knew how to work. I knew how to provide for myself. I never gave anyone a chance to do things for me because that also meant I was giving them a chance to let me down. From the age of 14, I always made sure that I had a job or some type of way to generate income. At the age of 31, God finally sat me down.

I was just a few months pregnant with my second son when I was told I had to be on complete bedrest with bathroom privileges only. Not only was I forced to leave my job, now I had to rely on my husband physically and financially. At that point, not listening would cost me my health and the health of my unborn child. The decision was a no-brainer, but that certainly did NOT make it easy. At that moment, I had no choice but to let go and let God. Do you know what

God did? He blew my mind! Not only did this situation provide me with a new level of trust and appreciation for my husband, I believe it also showed him that he was able to lead. My need to be in control is what prevented my husband from doing what God instructed him to do. How could he follow God's instruction to lead if I never followed God's instruction to submit? My stubborn ways, fear, and generational curses were the only factors preventing him from doing his job. At that point, it all became clear. Submission was only an issue for me when I looked at what I had to give up. The reward in submission was never explained to me.

When I submit, I am trusting him to be the head and make decisions that bring respect, clarity, and growth back to our marriage. As my husband is submitting to God, he vows to show me the same love that Christ showed the church. Jesus died on the cross for the sins of everyone to come. That kind of sacrifice and love is what my husband is tasked with showing me. I get to be loved in the same manner that Christ loved the church?! Sign me up! So, the next time you turn your nose up at the idea of having to submit to your spouse, know that God gave each of you roles that are equally challenging, yet rewarding, regarding the success of your marriage.

Today I invite you to seek God concerning the area of submission. Say This Prayer:

Lord I thank you for loving the church and for giving my spouse and I an example to follow. Forgive me for not being open to submission. Show me how to submit to my spouse and you. Allow submission to become a part of my daily routine so that it is no longer a task and becomes something I feel honored to do. In Jesus' Name, Amen.

Declaration: I HAVE RELEASED ALL NEGATIVE THOUGHTS I HAVE ASSOCIATED WITH THE WORD SUBMIT AND I WILL SUBMIT DAILY TO MY SPOUSE IN THE AREAS GOD INTENDED FOR ME TO

_____

_____

_____

_____

_____

_____

_____

_____

_____

Day 13: Intimacy

Under no circumstances should intimacy only exist in the bedroom. Many women are not even interested in what you have in mind for the bedroom if the intimacy is not there prior. Forever is a LONG time. Dates are not just for the engagement and honeymoon phase. You should be consistently and uniquely finding ways to be intimate with your spouse. Fall in love with the journey of your marriage. God intended for sex to be a sacred thing for just married couples. However, I am real enough to say that everyone does not wait that long. My son was in my wedding, so no judgment here! But what I will say is this. I understand why that was God's intent. If all you have is sex as your form of intimacy, what do you have when that is no longer available? What keeps your marriage spicy? What keeps you enticed about your spouse? What makes you want only them? Interestingly enough, this is one area that couples feel like they cannot talk to God about.

How often do you talk to God about the intimacy in your marriage? Did you ever consider how God feels about intimacy? Maybe looking into that will encourage you to feel more comfortable submitting your thoughts to Him about it.

Today I invite you to seek God concerning the intimacy in your marriage. Say this prayer:

Lord, I thank you for my marriage. Forgive me for taking advantage of what you have blessed me with. I know that your desire for us is to have a union based on your word. Today, I ask that you give me a strong intimate desire for my spouse. Allow us to work endlessly to show our love and passion for one another. Let us continue to fall in love each moment that we are intimately joined and continue to bless us as we draw nearer to each other and you. In Jesus' name, AMEN.

Declaration: I HAVE A HEALTHY INTIMATE DESIRE
FOR MY SPOUSE THAT GROWS DAILY

_____

_____

_____

_____

_____

_____

_____

_____

_____

Day 14: Communication

We were given two ears and one mouth for a reason. Listen twice as much as you speak. The place where most couples go wrong is that they listen to respond instead of listening to understand. Communication is everything to a marriage. Are you happy? Have you felt offended by something I have done? Are you being fulfilled? Do the kids need anything? Can we discuss how things are going financially? The same way you should check-in about feelings, check-in in general. It costs you nothing to listen to a person and be sensitive to their responses.

Most importantly, never make your spouse feel that they are wrong for expressing themselves. Once a person feels like they are a burden, it is typically hard for them to decide to speak up again. Do your best to make them feel comfortable enough to have a conversation with you whenever they feel they need to.

More importantly, switch up what you are talking about. I believe that communication becomes an issue when the topics do not change. Everything does not have to be about the kids, money, work, or other serious topics. Get to know your spouse on a deeper level than just the surface. Ask questions that make them think and stir up curiosity. Here are a few things to consider asking your spouse:

What would your ideal day look like? If money were not an issue at this moment, what three things would you purchase? How do you want to be remembered? Do you believe you are hard on yourself? If so, why? What is one hobby or activity you have always wanted to try?

These are simple questions that you can ask, not only to learn more about your spouse but also to have them think more about themselves. *whispers* It also helps you plan out special date nights secretly and "just because" gifts, too *wink*.

Today, seek God about the communication in your relationship. Say this prayer:

Lord, I thank you for a mouth to speak and ears to hear. I ask today for the discernment to know which to use at any given time. Remove any distractions that will set out to disrupt the flow of communication in our marriage. Give us the confidence to speak boldly and openly about anything that may be of importance to us. Help us never run out of things to say to each other and never stop wanting to learn about each other. Allow us to leave each conversation feeling accomplished and knowing that we made progress. In Jesus' name, Amen.

Declaration: I AM AN EFFECTIVE COMMUNICATOR

_____

_____

_____

_____

_____

_____

_____

_____

_____

Day 15: Boundaries

I have an exercise that I want you to try. It is tough, so I need you to brace yourself. Sit straight up, take a deep breath, and with all your power, say this word: "NO." I know, you were expecting more. But there is no more that needs to be said. Learning the art of NO will save your marriage and, ultimately, your life. No, I cannot break plans with my spouse just this one time because it is the only time you are available. No, I cannot loan you money. No, I cannot just have you as a friend knowing the relationship we had in the past. No, I do not want you to update me on what my EX is doing. No, I am not comfortable with you touching me there. No, I cannot watch your children for you. No, I cannot let you stay with me. No, I cannot lie for you. Boundaries. It is not mean, you do not have to explain yourself, and you should not feel bad. If your first thought is no or in the back of your mind, you are saying no, then the answer is no. Boundaries protect you by establishing a clear understanding of what is acceptable for you and what is not. Having a lack of boundaries will open the flood gates and allow others to decide on your thoughts and feelings. It is easy to identify when a boundary has been crossed because it usually presents stress, anxiety, discomfort, resentment, or fear. The hardest part about this is that it is typically those closest to you that cause you to go astray from your initial thought. Knowing them personally and their needs or situations causes you to feel bad for them and make an exception. I dare you to consider, when is the last time you made an exception for YOURSELF?

An easy way to set boundaries is to ask yourself two essential questions. What am I responsible for? What am I not responsible for? Answer those questions with clarity. Having a parent who forced you to be responsible for your siblings as a kid does not make you responsible for them in their adult lives or any situations they may have gotten themselves into. Setting boundaries also means there must be a release in things you have allowed yourself to feel obligated to do based on others' interpretations of your purpose. Know your "WHY." If your attachment to that situation no longer benefits the season you are in, permit yourself to let it go. You owe it to yourself, your marriage, and your overall future.

Today, be encouraged to seek God regarding establishing boundaries. Say this prayer:

Lord, I thank you for placing me here for a purpose. Setting boundaries will assist me in living out that purpose. Guide me in knowing what boundaries to set that will keep me aligned with your purpose for my life. Remove anything that hinders this from moving forward. Give me the unapologetic release that I need to let go of anything that I was not assigned to. Grant me the discernment to recognize what keeps me from saying no and the strength to forgive myself in those areas. I thank you in advance for the peace that this will give me. In Jesus' name, AMEN.

Declaration: I HAVE BOUNDARIES SET BY GOD THAT NO MAN CAN BREAK

_____

_____

_____

_____

_____

_____

_____

_____

_____

Day 16: Love

We did not genuinely find love in our marriage until we found God in our marriage. God is love. So, I cannot discuss one without discussing the other. 1 John 4:16 reminds us that if we say we live in love, we must live in God. God gave his only Son to die for our sins as the ultimate sign of love and sacrifice. Love is respect; love is humility; love is selflessness; love is honor. For a moment, let us refer to 1 Corinthians 13:4-7. Replace the word "Love" with your name.

Love is patient; love is kind; love does not envy; love does not boast; love is not proud. Love does not dishonor others; love is not self-seeking; love is not easily angered; love keeps no record of wrongs. Love does not delight in evil but rejoices with the truth. Love always protects, love always trusts, love always hopes & love always perseveres.

Now, go and reread it and replace the word "Love" with the words "In My Marriage, We."

What did you discover? Are you patient? Are you kind? In your marriage, are you easily angered? In your marriage, do you always trust? Whatever you cannot answer "yes" to, should be the areas in which you strive to work harder. Every day will not be a great day, and every moment will not be a great moment, but if you keep the greater purpose in the forefront, you will succeed. Knowing that you each come into the marriage with different ideas of what love is, makes it difficult to show love in the same way. It also causes you to feel like you are doing enough because you are doing all you know how to do. So, you must rebuild what you know love to be and how it is shown. You must come together and create a dialect based on love that is custom to your marriage. Putting God in the center of your marriage makes it great. Keeping God at the center of your marriage makes it last!

Today, I encourage you to seek God in love and in your relationship with Him being that they are the same. Say this prayer:

God, I thank you for the love you show daily. I desire to draw nearer to you and to keep you in the center of my marriage. I want to show myself and my spouse the same agape love that you show to us all. Rebuild my heart concerning the topic of love. Remove anything that hinders me from showing love genuinely. Remind me that I must show your love not just in my words but also in my actions. Whenever I struggle in love, remind me of the greatest love ever shown, the sacrifice of your Son on the cross. Guide me in the areas that I fall short and give me clarity, where I may lack understanding. In Jesus' name, Amen.

Declaration: I HAVE THE LOVE OF GOD
AND I REFLECT THE LOVE OF GOD

_____

_____

_____

_____

_____

_____

_____

_____

_____

After 16 days of consistent devotion, prayers, and declarations, I pray that your seeds have landed in the fertile ground of your new foundation. I can tell you 8 million additional things to focus on, but you need to know one main important truth, Rebuilding Takes a Lifetime. The work is just beginning. Though I would like to believe that this book will give you everything you need, the real work happens IN your marriage. It happens in the application of everything that you have learned. It happens in your willingness to want to grow together.

It happens in your desire to seek God concerning your marriage. It happens when you decide to not be a statistic. It happens when you stop settling for mediocrity. It happens when you BELIEVE God for what He has promised you, and you take Him at his word. It happens when you let go and let God.

The Final Declaration

If someone told me that I would be the author of a book, specifically about marriage, I would completely disregard that statement. In fact, I did disregard that statement. In May of 2020, I received a prophetic word that I would be writing a book. I took everything to heart that was said EXCEPT that statement. In November 2020, I received the same prophetic word from a completely different person. This time it came after three straight days of having dreams about the contents of this book. I told God that if He intended for me to do this, He would have to give me the words. This book was written in 2 weeks. Suddenly, "Divorce-Limited" went from a TITLE about my marriage to a TESTIMONY about my marriage! I received an important lesson from this, and I would like to share it with you.

YOU matter. The main reason that I stressed the importance of finding who YOU are is because you are someone beyond titles. I am no expert on marriage, and I am no counselor; I am no ordained minister. However, I am someone with experience in all these topics who is no longer afraid to share. My experiences helped me to write this book, not my titles. My insight matters. My prayers matter. My testimony matters. My WHOLE testimony matters. There is someone who may be saying, "why would she put her business out there like that?" There are two simple answers to that question. First, someone else's breakthrough was attached to the "YES," I gave God when I agreed to write this book. If even ONE marriage is changed or ONE life is saved, I have done my job. And second, I made it through. A lot of people are afraid to take a leap of faith because they do not know anyone personally who was at their lowest point and made it out. I am here to be that person for you. My husband and I had a union in 2013, a ceremony in 2014 and a vow renewal in 2019 and NONE of that helped us. Nothing changed until WE changed. We decided to be better. We decided to become whole then fix our marriage. We decided to keep God at the center of our lives. Now, we have a constant reminder that if God bought us out of this, He would indeed work miracles in any other area of our lives.

I am beyond words with an appreciation for you taking the time to read my story. You are now a part of my journey. When this book becomes a bestseller (C'MON DECLARATION!) I can look back and say it was because of God first but also you. You felt my words were important enough to purchase this book. You felt my experiences were worth reading. You felt that my gift was worth supporting. And for that, I say Thank You.

I gave you 16 different declarations to speak over yourself and your marriage. Now, here is MY declaration for you:

I Decree and Declare that

God is at the center of your marriage and your life

Your experiences matter

Your journey matters

Your boundaries matter

Your mindset matters

Your heart matters

Your testimony matters

You do know who you are

Submission is something you are honored to do

Seeds were planted on fertile soil

You have clarity

You have understanding

You have peace

You have joy

You have God Strength

The Word of the Lord lives within you

The Holy Spirit guides and protects you

Your marriage is ordained by God

Your marriage will be a success

You are on one accord

Faithfulness is normal in your marriage

Honesty is normal in your marriage

Respect is normal in your marriage

Genuine Agape Love is normal in your marriage

Forgiveness is normal in your marriage

Negativity in any form has no place in your life

The enemies' plans will never prosper

Supernatural blessings have reached your doorstep

You have re-evaluated

You have repaired

You have replaced

You have rebuilt

And...the chances of your marriage ending in Divorce...are... LIMITED.

In Jesus Name, AMEN.

Reflections

_____

_____

_____

_____

_____

_____

_____

_____

_____

_____

_____

_____

_____

_____

_____

_____

_____

_____

_____

Jasmine Carey-Crowner

About the Author

JASMINE CAREY-CROWNER was born on May 24th in Berlin, Germany. Her family moved to Maryland in the early 90s. She was educated in the Anne Arundel County Public School System and was a 2006 graduate of Old Mill Senior High in Millersville, Maryland. After beginning her higher education at Coppin State University, Jasmine pursued her lifelong passion for Cosmetology. From this, she obtained a Senior Cosmetology License. In 2010 she met her now, husband, and they welcomed their first child in 2012. In 2016, Jasmine became the owner of JSC Events and turned her passion for all things creative and hospitable into a successful business. That same year, she became Co-Chair of the Young Adult Ministry at her church. From this position, she developed a stronger love for young adults and a love for cultivating healthy relationships between young adult couples. After an exceedingly difficult pregnancy, she and her husband welcomed their second child in 2020. Two months later, due to a Global Pandemic, she was forced to leave her job with the State of Maryland, where she specialized in Estate Planning to care for her children and family permanently. During this time, she re-branded her business and began to fully live the life God had been calling her to live. She is known to many as a jack of all trades. At any time, she may be designing an event, decorating a wedding, operating her photobooth, servicing a hair or permanent makeup client, creating custom journals, or setting up a yard card display. No matter what gift or talent she is currently pursuing, you can be SURE that she is somewhere putting a smile on someone's face. Now, Jasmine has turned her passion for hospitality into a love for encouraging and strengthening the relationships of everyone she encounters. "Divorce-Limited" is the first of many efforts to bring hope, insight, and restoration to relationships everywhere.